THE RESILIENCE

A collection of Poems to express, inspire
and keep the spirit driven

Diana Melhet

This small collection of poems would not have been possible without the challenges of the corporate world, the endless support and patience of my family and friends and the belief my partner had in me.
This book is meant to inspire the reader to continue to fight the good fight and keep the candle burning.

CONTENTS

Title Page — 1

Dedication — 7

Index — 9

About The Author — 63

To Katie and my parents

INDEX

- Here we go again
- I've learned to Live
- Finding the resilience
- Someday I'll fly
- The last part of Darkness
- And then there's a tomorrow
- The underachievers' club
- Lost...
- Silly me
- Monotonous
- Incessant Rambling
- Proud and Arrogant!
- To be or not to be
- The Arian's march
- The stars, my friends
- Looking for the rainbow
- I wish I was better than this
- The goodnight song
- But the horse has to die
- Invisible chain
- Losing sleep
- With you, my friend
- Walking on broken glass
- At a loss for words
- Be that rainbow!
- Before the end
- As the world turns cold

- Seething
- Light at the end of tunnel

Here We Go Again

It's that time of the year, when everybody celebrates
When it all comes to the end, and here we go again
The things that everybody does, we never seem to do
It's no more fun to roam about, we're getting stuck in the blue

Some memories were bitter, we took a pinch of salt
And the good ones, we had real fun, and remembered Galt

Hoping for a better year and we hope for something new
We hope that things will change now and hope we start anew
Try to ignite that fire we try to find that spark,
The winter here was pretty bad, the snow wiped it out

With courage I move forward and with grit I grind my teeth
The fist is clenched and bleeds blood and the brow forms a V
I take a pledge and decide with resilience I'll strike back
I won't let anything faze me, with patience I'll attack

The bad things were a good riddance and the good was not so great
Glad to move on ahead and now with Janus we shake
The lessons we learnt were not so great, for more we do yearn
The more we try to get, the more we do discern

With hope filled in my heart, I take my blithe step
Towards the light that's promising and I'm all set
Let's celebrate the past, the things that's best forgotten
And usher in the new year and walk the paths not trodden

I've learned to Live

Along came I, with nothing to lose
When there were simpler things to choose,
But life grows and moves ahead
And difficult becomes fun instead

Weirdness and uneasiness go hand in hand sometimes
When you try to judge someone but end up part of crime
Break does expectations and shatter does the dream
Without a sound you learn to weep, with a smile you learn to scream

Clenching fist hide the anger 'cause in my pocket is my hand
The tears flow with the rain and nobody understands

You learn to live with cruelty, the world at first it seems
The sorrow's buried deep within, you see it in your dreams
Now that it's been a long time, unreal it seems to me
That I smile with the world and have forgotten broken things
Have learnt to live away from all, though company I do keep
I laugh and talk but I do remember, I am what I need

Now with a chip on my shoulder, wandering 'bout this road
I need nobody beside me, I'm better off alone
I need no shoulder to cry on or hands when I'm in dark
No voice to care for me, I shun this world's facade
I don't care about their advices, I don't care about the games
I'll be damned to get affected, it doesn't matter what you say

This I've learnt to live with, and have longed to be this free
Alone I am and will be and when it's over I'll be in peace.

Finding the resilience

Drowning in the pit of inaction's paralyze
Engulfing darkness exploding into thousands of vague mirage
Creeps in desperation, but I am the strength seeker
The pit is not deep enough, instead I now dig deeper

Alone I am and want to be, the sins are mine to bear
Not lonely and making solitary retreat, perpetual frown I wear
Invisible cross I carry, 'cross the life's street
Is it delirium I'm experiencing or with pain I do really meet

The moon sets as the night's glory rests in peace
The rays penetrate the darkness; dispels everything weak
This satchel's my baggage, a constant that's with me
Weighing me down as I walk, a burden, a part of me.

The fury burns within, potency grows to speak
The reckless part I cut it off and throw into the sea
That part is what I hated, I will not reminisce
The peeled knees will get me through this abhorrent journey

This knot in my mind is untied to pave way for more to learn
These boundaries that are self proclaimed be felled with a loud thud
Now I spend my waking hours, trying to wake up
The flowers I crushed on my way, I'm trying to make it up

Now I find my darkness, in the shadow I see the light
I see the view in front of me, I found what was right
I thank my stars above; I've been saved from the blight
Prepare I will ahead, the resilience's back to fight

With might in my thoughts, my pride now sits upright

DIANA MELHET

With armor in my hand, and vision in my sight
I'm out to seek my destiny, the one I'll write myself
Reason's the totem I've discovered, of the end no longer afraid!

Someday I'll fly

Unaware, I fly, the winds take me high
This horizon's new, so is surreal sky
Transcend new boundaries, test new winds
Ignorance rests as I flutter my wings

Birds of a feather, lost in the weather
Not a clue about the rule or the sun
But the birds are tough and glad together
Can get the things they want, done.

My seeking is unique; distance, inevitable
I am what I need, taking chance is debatable
Gambled I have with caution and heart
Tangled in a mosaic of interests and scars

There's no answer to the gaping questions
Those haven't been forgotten, but never been asked
I wonder about the petty confessions
And wander about abandoned paths

I'll need some time to think this through
To swallow and stomach distasteful rue
These wings will get me strong again
I'll master the pyrotechnics one day

'cross the mountains, past the sky
I'll fly right; zoom past over July
I'll fly above the clouded gloom
Where the tears don't fall; above the hues

My blood and tears will have earned the price

DIANA MELHET

I'll be at peace, when I close my eyes.

The last part of Darkness

They told me to take the leap,
They drove me off the cliff
Blindfolded and bound, terror within
All I had was zilch

No sight or leverage I have,
It's just a clue I seek,
They mistook my swollen and bleeding back,
For their sword's sheath

Wavering and losing balance,
I feel the narrow ledge,
I remember the times of my life,
Moments filled with regrets,

Uneventful though it was,
I'm glad that part's done,
The one that could not be,
And the ones you wanted none

The nights when I used to sleep,
And ones that were blurred,
Between them and the day ahead,
Was the nightmare I preferred

I guess the fear's dead,
Soon with it I'll meet, Couldn't live
Without when I was awake,
Can't abandon when I'm asleep

Here I am waiting,
it'll be my turn soon

DIANA MELHET

Apathy's what I'm feeling,
It came when I needed it to.

And then there's a tomorrow

The eyes have grown tired
Though the fire's still awake
Inquisitive I aspire
Today may not be the day

The todays are busy
Living in the moment we say
The exercises far too many
For bread we must pay

The muscles are flexed and raw
They ache a little too
Where's the fun without a challenge
Say bring it on, will do

We'll struggle again today
For battles we must fight
The trials and tribulations
Will throw the right light

The mistakes must be made
The lessons to be learnt
The fire must be played with
And fingers must be burnt

Experience we must all
The present day's fruits
The deep hidden disappointments
What's false and what's the truth?

And then there's a tomorrow
This was just today

DIANA MELHET

The things I thought were done for good, will be done again

Tomorrow a new day
A day none have seen
A day I would never miss
Isn't a night I wouldn't dream.

The underachievers' club

Hardwork we fear not, for we toil night and day,
Subordination of interests, forgoing all the play,
We gladly skip breakfast, Inefficient we are dubbed,
Little do we achieve, we're The Underachiever's club

Sometimes we miss a point, perhaps a whole page,
Sitting in the dark, working, fuming with rage,
Perhaps what we do is not how it's done,
Hours put in relentlessly toiling in the sun.

Peace of mind, we say, is what we live for,
Exhaustion sinks in, on the psyche takes a toll,
The work still remains let alone appreciation,
The world shrinks in, remains only villainous trepidation.

We lose sleep over things left undone,
Dissatisfied, incompetent, eyes better unopened,
But the dawn must break, so must we,
Brave that we are, we start, resilience the key.

Lost...

Lost in never ending abyss
Leaves me groping for hope
Cost of wishing the end,
May leave me battling more.

Being able to want and wanting to be able,
The things never heard of, but lost in the label,
Misreading and vagueness pave way for more disguise,
Unfathomable clues, arduous fake paradise.
Better off on earth, than the strenuous path to pointlessness,
Questioning the worth, to leave the dreams I once had, but then
Lost is the time and the spirit divine,
Fading away to black, who knows what's destined
But toil we must, bear the mild yoke they say,
The atlas can't lend the earth to anyone any day,
But what if the blood spilt is gone to waste,
What if the pain doesn't subside when they take,
My life, now that's all I have to do,
and undo to make it in time left for doom
Wading through the muck, grinding in the grief,
The day itself so long
But the years they call it brief

The fog covers my path,
My eyes blinded by fear
The numbness a quiet relief
Left are no more tears

So where do we go from here?
Is the fog even meant to clear?
What was it that was supposed to be, and the things that were dear?

Questions unanswered hope nowhere near,
Somehow there's still courage left to tread deeper from here

This too shall pass
They always say,
Pass when I ask, arise.
Perhaps, burning is the only way out, I surmise.

Silly me

From the dark recesses of my mind,
Crept a flicker of light,
How could I be so naive to think this would end the blight
Perhaps it's a lighted match,
That'll be blown off soon
Perhaps it's just a spark
Ray of hope? A boon?

Silly me, I thought these were changing times
Silly me, I thought the fallen me would rise,
Silly me, I let myself think beyond hope
Silly me, I almost smiled, too much here to cope.

Things going wrong, doesn't let me catch my breath
On a song, the beat's on filled with regret
I've been through the wringer,
Matters little, the pain's the same
The grind excruciating, the efforts, vain.

Silly me, I thought this was to end
Silly me, too many broken pieces to mend
Silly me, claustrophobic once, dreams of coffin
Silly me, Every couple of breath needs morphine

Blood sweat tears, time, health, not enough
There's probably more need, this road too rough
Through the tourniquet I bleed,
Threatening to bite the dust,
But on I go, 'cause for more I lust

Silly me, this road seemed glistening
Of gold, silly me, I wasn't listening, back then when I was told,

Silly me, the blood drained, tears dried up now what
They still seem to think more to offer I've got

Pointless, no direction, waiting for a cue,
The silly me, wants out, silliness posing the truth,
The blame's gone, no pointing fingers alone,
Silly me wants this king dethroned,

It doesn't matter What I say, really, do you believe me?
Or will you wave me off
Cos it's just me, the silly me?

Monotonous

How many times do I get over
How many times do I begin,
It's crazy test this life,
How many times do I dream?

They say don't be afraid to dream
when the dream's 'round the corner
But I'm flying the opposite direction
Have crossed all the borders

The borders of certainty,
the one that was secure
That one that lead to nothing,
But where I knew where I was

What strange journey is this?
The one I can't comprehend.
The one where I am to work,
The one where I am to pretend

Maybe I should have stuck to the road
The one at corners which bends
There's anticipation of happiness
Opportunities to swoop it tends

But here I am, crumbling
dying under the weight on my shoulder
But still I stand, for the Atlas must
Bear with the burden and molder

I breathe, stay low, to the stomach I'm sick
How much longer before I can sit

tick tock tick tock tick tock tick
I think it is time, about time I'll exit!!

Incessant Rambling

Shut up brain, shut up heart,
This is not the place to start
Relax and stop thinking now
Let numbness smother things that are

Perhaps tomorrow be the day,
Perhaps never as they say
Why bother what happens, it's my pride
And numbness I have by my side.

Losing sleep doesn't count,
Waking up matters now
Endless wasted moments before I bow
What resulted in a shattered crown

Building bridges just to burn,
Withheld inhibitions inside it swirls
Fuming, consuming thoughts arrive
Taking my sleep in its stride

I hate to have them back today,
On my way to sleep haven
Why do you raise your wicked head
Stir up confusion instead

Let me sleep go back you thoughts
My heart isn't ideal landing spot
I'll brush them away instantly
Time to take one more morphine

Then I fall unconscious me
Fists clenched constantly

Waking up, I feel alive
Fists unclenched but not relieved

Shut up brain, shut up heart
What you say is miles apart
One too sorrow in recluse
Other too cheerful, to be true

Fairly level headed not me
Afraid to tread now in between
Too forward or conservative
I'll find the middle ground superlative

There's no reason for dichotomy
Both have best interests for me,
When they're one, the heart and brain
There's nothing which I can't obtain

The possibility of such a thing,
Is what makes us wish, makes me dream
Defy them all, on a wing,
Unachievable, no such thing.

There we go, the train of thoughts,
The pouring of the mind distraught,
The fire's ignited, 't has to last,
Leave the doubts in the past.

Proud and Arrogant!

Proud and arrogant riding the wave,
If I fall down, I'll just get up again,
This world is just stable for a fleeting moment
This surfboard my mate, someday, might not go with

The time passes and now I walk,
This road that climbs up miles in the dark,
Towards the light I cannot see,
There will be sunshine, I do believe

Alone as I came, alone I'll go
Fighting the battles for they 're mine to blow
Fire in belly, fierce my pride,
Manifestation of the storm inside,

Here I go, always armored up
Striding my way, clamored up
Soul that screams for things they say
I don't need yours I make my own way.

To be or not to be

To be or not to be
To breathe or not to breathe
Which path unfolding to be chosen
The green or not so green?

I speak as I ought to speak
I dream as I ought to dream
Somewhere the world turns topsy turvy
I scream as I ought to scream

I run but I lose the race
I'd rather stride my way
Still a rat, in the game
I'd rather make my day

Distant numb today
I had my time in breeze
Now all gone away
I'm down but then there's more beneath

Be deceived or pretend to be
Not sure, let go of the trapeze
Clutching the loose bricks
I climb
Is it me or am I going down deep

Should I feel what I ought to feel
A foolish fool for my dreams
Drowning in the deepest seas
Of lights I dream and I see

Is it real as real it can be

Or beyond the realm it feels
Should it matter, shouldn't wouldn't
Couldn't help my heart it's free

Was it freedom that I desired?
Was it comfort that was meant to be?
Why do I miss the water
Doesn't make sense any

Do I know what I want to be?
Or where or who's for me?
Can I speak what I ought to speak?
Can I dream what I ought to dream?

Can I sing as I ought to sing?
With the voice that's deep within
Waiting for a sign from up above
Maybe I'll breathe as I ought to breathe.

The Arian's march

Dreams to be seen, dreams to be lived
Dreams to be dared, dreams to fulfill
Daring to fly, hoping to soar
Wishing upon that star below
Loving so deep, caring so much
Touching the hearts, getting that rush
Unconditional it is, nothing to lose
Only to gain, here with you
Thankful I am, grateful for time
Nowhere else I'd be, here I am
Walking ahead, going so slow,
Sprinting in a jiffy, it's me you know
Dreaming a dream, living in the clouds
Not backing down, head full of doubts
Still I fly, testing my wings
Uncharted grounds, uncharted winds
so much more, left to do
But rest I must that's best for you
Tomorrow's the time for another kill
Another battle, another will
Discovering self, recovering heart
Resilient minds, shining in the dark
On we go, forward we thrust
With fierce fire and courage in us.

The stars, my friends

The stars come out
For they need me
To be my friend
For they miss me

I will tell them
The events befallen
The moments found
And those forgotten

I'll tell them how
I had my day
About my plans
For they will stay

They all blink
Sleepy I think
But they share
About things they care
And so do I
I'm their friend, aren't I?

Some too sleepy
Dream world bound
Crash to the ground
Ray of light astound

I close my eyes
Pray for them
All the wellness
At their helm

As we resume
The talks of town
The tears and joys
The feelings unbound

Millions of shoulders
All for me
Millions of comforts
Everything I seek

With lifted weights
I find my peace
Bid adieu to the stars
For being with me

Till the next day
Comes to pass
With more to listen
More to laugh

But for now
I'll call it a night
To my million friends
I bid goodnight.

DIANA MELHET

Looking for the rainbow

Looking for that rainbow
Searching everyday
Need a little sunshine
Need a little rain
Sometimes the sun
Hides behind the clouds
Sometimes the sun
Dispels everything around
But the rainbow's formed
When they both meet
With a little bit of sunshine
A light drizzle greets
But there is a constant
Struggle for peace
One overlooks
The other oversees
Will I ever know?
Will it ever show?
Will the darkness be overcome with the right glow?
With the right balance
The colors come out
Yellow and grey give way
To the bright vibgyor
Looking at the wet sky
Seeing no sign
Waiting another day
Waiting another night

I wish I was better than this

I wish I was better
Better equipped and fast
I wish I was better
And can do things that last

Instead I'm left wandering
Wondering at the stars
Why do they seem to wink
And why are they so far?

Why could I not figure
What I'm supposed to do?
Instead I'm left trying
At something everyone is good

But where's my part written?
Why can I not read?
I'm trying hard to listen
But no one seems to speak

I wish I was stronger
To take on more of the blame
Some part of it was not my fault
But now it's all a shame

Wish I could see the stumbling blocks,
Before I fall on those
Wish I had seen a bit ahead
Instead of staring at my toes

I wish I could tell them
How I see through their lies

DIANA MELHET

How I feel about their tears
And all their fake smiles

I wish I was better
At what my heart yearns
A skill that I'd enjoy
A skill that would earn

Keep your eyes and ear
Open wide, they said
You will learn a lot from that
I did, I'm afraid.

What you learn can shock you
It can make you wise
I choose to look elsewhere
And at things without disguise

The search will continue
A constant effort and will
A will to make a difference
An effort to build the skill.

The goodnight song

It's time to stop, time to breathe
Stop running, it's time I slept
Ran hard as I could
Now catching my breath
It's time to stop
Watching my step

The bones then clutter
Slowly rumble
With pride I began
Then slowly humbled
It's time for this one
To rest and sleep
To turn into a lion
From being a sheep

The resilience comes
After the fall
Where one ends,
New chapters evolve
But now I close my eyes
And dream
Of stars and skies and
Happy things
And pray the lord
To give me sight
To wield my pen
And spread the light.

DIANA MELHET

But the horse has to die

A dreary path and rustic breeze
To this I didn't agree
For speed and strength I'm sought
After all, I am that horse

The one who befriends the rider
And goes on without a sigh
Even when the sands are wider
Than what seems, the sky

I push my limits ahead
No complains, no pit stops
My friend my master forgets
Soon all shall be lost

Enter: the camel, made for dunes
My fellow, my counter part,
He groans and grieves and makes the halt,
When he thinks he should stop

He goes on for days and nights
For he's accepted and well rested
Now I struggle to take a step
My limits are well tested

A traitor, they say, as I drop
Drop down on my knees
What good a horse that knows not
Itself, if forgets to breathe

The rider's friend, companion
Shall now be bid goodbye

The rider will survive
But the horse has to die.

Invisible chain

Twisting and turning
With my thoughts unsettled
Like a very hot fire
Under a burning kettle

These ideas, they stew, they boil and they cook
At the end of my wits, everywhere I've looked
A way is what I need right now, one desperate move
Or it will be checkmate again guessing nothing new

I refuse to go down without a fight
Most certainly I refuse to go down
I may hide, find ways to bide my time
Soul searching, this soul is well bestowed

At times I falter, I fall down
Get bogged by invisible chains
These chains that tie my thoughts and heart,
my hands and legs and brain

They seem impossible to be unshackled
How can I begin to try?
Among the ridicule and cruel heckle
It makes me want to cry

It makes me want to give up
this fight, You, can have it all
All the mud slings gory
All the glory and awards

But something stirs inside
How can I let it be?

How can I let myself be trapped
With bitter memories?

How can something as trivial
As bitter conjectures
Shackle everything I know
Time for my deflector

These imaginary bonds
Shall be put to test
All Chinese whispers and whisperers
Shall be put to rest

And all the demons in my head
All of them will be slayed
They say it is a nightmare
Of dreams I'm not afraid

It's time to take a silent moment
With conviction I must move
Not let this break my swagger
This moment I shall use

To rise above the clouds
My own standards be surpassed
Things need to be set right
In stone nothing's cast.

Losing sleep

I never thought I would lose my sleep
But all these thoughts I cannot keep,
Inside, my head there's a thunderstorm,
That rains on hope and thoughts warm.

Craving for a little piece of sunshine,
As darkness envelops my delirious mind
A ray of hope, a symbol or sign
Maybe only intervention divine

Can save me now, for the bugle's sounded
The chip on my shoulder, is fairly astounded
through this wringer I must go again,
A war of rules, clash of minds restrained

A fairly average game to lose,
I so did not want my life confused,
Where is that star I used to see,
Alas the sky is growing weak,

I look across the horizons spread
The stars they fade, there's the sun instead
How long have I been gazing by
And searched in the wrong part of the sky

How long have I been pushing the bend,
The dead end I didn't think to mend
My ways, I missed the turn somewhere,
Looking back and the darkness glares

Destiny they say are made by choices,
When silence gets replaced by voices,

The decision now has to be made,
To stare the wall, or gaze the ray

Of sunlight that marks my new way
Maybe this will take me away
From the dread, that's filled up to the seams
Maybe one night will help me sleep

DIANA MELHET

With you, my friend

Don't worry my friend,
For life sometimes
May seem to let you down

Don't worry my friend
For the wind may chime
A tune that makes you frown

The path descends
Ahead in time
Some hold your hand, too strong

But then instead
Of joy sublime
They may take back the crown

Fear not; tread
Slow, with open eyes
Your path unique as this song

Their choices lead
To leave your side
Some more may come along

It's true, my friend
I will not bide
My time with you; is long.

With you I spend
My hours, my life,
With you is where I belong

With you; in trend
Of falls and strides
With all cheek and tongue

The times won't bend
The bond and pride
We brave it all as one

The time will mend
For lost time
The frolic and the fun

Together we'll fend
Off the harsh tides
The battles shall be won

Don't worry my friend
I'm on your side
The ride has just begun!

❖ ❖ ❖

Walking on broken glass

Wavered faith and darkened past
Makes me walk on broken glass
It is by choice, it's how I voice
Some right actions for some wrong past

It all started with one wrong move
One lesson less learned in school
One path easy, one way hard
One called to me, other seemed far

I chose the familiar, saw known faces
It doesn't take time, time it erases
All the faith I seemingly had
Now, how much can I understand

Broken vows and forgotten pledge
Brings me closer to the edge
Just when I'm about to fall
I seem to have a good recall

The path now seems to fade away
T'was only one from which I swayed
The broken bottles on the way
Must walk back, with brittle pace,

The path untrodden may not be wrong
If only the little voice had been strong,
But now, as all is said and done
The voice be heeded and things undone

A difficult tread back to the start,
But now I will not lose heart,

The demons shall be put to rest,
And the weight be lifted off my chest!

At a loss for words

So much inside me
Beneath it stirs
But strangely I find me
At a loss for words

Sometimes silent
Like a saint
At times violent
Mighty rage

Comes out in different forms
And hurts
But I find myself at a loss for words
It has been too long

That I've written a prose
Started so many
Then my heart froze
Witty got pitiful, the city got cold

But I'm still at a loss for words
The feelings are lodged
In a heart chamber, locked
Trying out all keys

Maybe I'll just knock
The letters approach the door then blur
Once again, at a loss for words
They used to be my lone strength

At will I would make egos bend
But now the eerie silence creeps

In their search I travel deep within
Maybe someday they will again surge

But for now, I'm at a loss for words
I hope I crack this labyrinth
With some luck, maybe a shady hint
A crazy insight, a secret path
A steady journey and a bloody lint
We will meet soon, where words won't end
Where heart is empty and eyes don't lament
But till such time, a cost to be occurred
For I am, truly, at a loss for words.

Be that rainbow!

When music lifts you at the end of day
The sky is overcast but you make hay
Elevated in this downtrodden world
When things don't come your way you learn
These moments of magic then paves the way
There seems to be no apparent change
The eyes when closed, the heart smiles
The melodies on which my life rides
The beat on which I walk again
The lyrics, everything I want to say
A silent acknowledgement of what I feel
How steady knowledge went from these streets
No more room for no complaints
No expectation, no pain, no gain
No highs to reach, no lows to fall
Only skies, to see and mine to call
Only time can be my friend and foe
Forget everything and start with hope
I reconcile the cranky child in me
So much more to learn and seek
Why bother with all the hopeless vain
Thoughts that bring me down again
Why not choose the exciting path
Where glory would be built to last
Why not see the sun in clouds
Why can't light be in darkness found
Why not hope to live some more
Why not smile and laugh from core
Why not sing and dance in mirth
Why not make this time worth?
Nothing lasts? That's a lie!
This moment lasted for a lifetime

So many lives yet to be lived
So many chances to be seized
So what if today it poured and rained
Shine! Be that rainbow and bless it came.

Before the end

The road of maze on which I walk
It twists and turns around
In store I have a lot of rage
But ignorant and happy I sound

The invisible thorns I walk upon
They pierce the cheery soul
The mud that splashes all around
They soil the heart of stone

Can see the setting sun ahead
But I must walk on some more
To be the man I think I am
I must pursue this lore

The legs froze in its wake
So stiff, my brain has frozen
This is something I can't shake
Maybe this is the moment chosen

Indeed we know how it all ends
But I must suffer some more
Till I'm scraped away, I've lent
My limbs left to be torn

Maybe the maze will be solved
I might spot an exit
Or way too much I'll get involved
And it's too late to forfeit

As long as the blood and sweat
And tears don't dry my soul

The mind perseveres till last breath
I'll go on, till I'm not told.

Seething

The crusty voices, underlying mistrust
Cushioned in laughter and playfulness
A shallow sporadic voice that bursts
What comes after is venom as jest

You're fooling none, I know this game
Understand the friction, shades of grey
What I've become, what this became
We pan the diction, needle in bale

A foot soldier marching on today
Over the hill, over the fire
Across the river, inside the maze
Knowing a trap, follow the sire

What good is a rant that can't be heard?
If thoughts are stifled and Hands tied
Dense smoke that comes with mirror,
Shards of glass swallowed with pride

I fight, I fight the indignant fight
Inside my head a storm brews
Outside are rainbows and butterflies
My demeanor, sharp and cool

This has to stop the seething rage
That grows inside this caged Bird
Face I must or simply walk away
This rising wave must not be curbed.

For I might lose the inner voice
The discerner of black and white

The toughest war rages within
When soul and mind stir up a fight

Another way, a clearer path
Alternatives must be found tonight
For I may not rise if I fall,
My freedom is my own device

As the world turns cold

A nick, a nudge, so quick to judge
Can't be careful, pressure's too much
Blatant blame, as egos touch
Better pack a punch, Don't think as such

Stepping on toes, drawing first bows
Don't think twice, no peace restored,
Indecency is acceptable, Cheating is smart
Pushing things on another is the only way to start

As this world turns cold, spite turns bold
Hate turns stronger, love gets told
Politeness walked upon, sad and stowed
Waiting for a spark that's expected to mold

The likes that trample on bodies and souls
To stand up for one, in spite of what's sold,
I'd rather be thought of as meek and old
Then the smart ones, as the story unfolds

The gory details will swallow you whole,
When these gallows completely shake your core,
Remember, despite being hurt and sore,
Stand your ground, reinforcement in store

I'm going through changes, like Em and Oz
Rough edges rounded, but I hit the pause,

I reflect back as I feel my frozen hands
Leaden head with an evasive stance
I scream, yell, but glide the way through
Make new way for the latest recruit!

DIANA MELHET

Light at the end of tunnel

Key to my ki
Everything from the heart
East to my west
Right where we are

Time's never been better
Hear them haters roar
All the stars spar
Now, align themselves more

A silent inner voice
Is calm and steady
Weary of the battles, but;
Into the light we're heading

Little bit of sunshine
Little bit of rain
Art of the balance
Love this black and gray

Where the soul smiles
As it meets the match
Yesterday, it seems like
Sparks, they're still intact

Leap in faith, with me
On the journey ahead
Veritable selves, we'll see
Everything with a clear head

Yester years gone
Our time now, is reality

Usurper of my heart, I love thee!

ABOUT THE AUTHOR

Diana Melhet

Diana, an introvert, had the habit of penning down small poems, whenever she felt that the routine job was coming up with disappointments or was too challenging to continue with. It was her way of keeping herself motivated and going headstrong in the corporate world.
A self proclaimed slow learner, Diana started writing in 2010 as a pastime that slowly developed into a passion. She is from the suburbs of Mumbai and works in the financial services sector.
Diana Melhet is a pen name

www.ingramcontent.com/pod-product-compliance
Lightning Source LLC
Chambersburg PA
CBHW061719130726
47996CB00006B/2397